Memories of a Lifetime™

Weddings

ARTWORK FOR SCRAPBOOK AND FABRIC-TRANSFER CRAFTS

Sandra Evertson

Sterling Publishing Co., Inc. New York
A Sterling/Chapelle Book

Author: Sandra Evertson
  www.ParisFleaMarketDesigns.com
  www.Shabbytiques.com

Contributing Designer: Mary C. Norman, Thanks mom!

If you have any questions or comments, please contact:
  Chapelle, Ltd., Inc., P.O. Box 9252, Ogden, UT 84409
  (801) 621-2777 • (801) 621-2788 Fax
  e-mail: chapelle@chapelleltd.com
  Web site: www.chapelleltd.com

PC Configuration: Windows 98 or later with 128 MB Ram or greater. At least 100 MB of free hard disk space. Dual speed or faster CD-ROM drive, and a 24-bit color monitor.

Macintosh Configuration: Mac OS 9 or later with 128 MB Ram or greater. At least 100 MB of free hard disk space. Dual speed or faster CD-ROM drive, and a 24-bit color monitor.

10 9 8 7 6 5 4 3 2

Published by Sterling Publishing Co., Inc.
387 Park Avenue South, New York, NY 10016
© 2005 by Sterling Publishing Co., Inc.
Distributed in Canada by Sterling Publishing
c/o Canadian Manda Group, 165 Dufferin Street
Toronto, Ontario, Canada M6K 3H6
Distributed in Great Britain by Chrysalis Books Group PLC,
The Chrysalis Building, Bramley Road, London W10 6SP, England
Distributed in Australia by Capricorn Link (Australia) Pty. Ltd.
P. O. Box 704, Windsor, NSW 2756, Australia
Printed and Bound in China
All Rights Reserved

Sterling ISBN 1-4027-2368-7

For information about custom editions, special sales, premium and corporate purchases, please contact Sterling Special Sales Department at 800-805-5489 or specialsales@sterlingpub.com.

Introduction

Imagine having hundreds of rare, vintage images right at your fingertips. With our *Memories of a Lifetime™* series, that's exactly what you get. We've scoured antique stores, estate sales, and other outlets to find one-of-a-kind images to give your projects the flair that only old-time artwork can provide. From Victorian postcards to hand-painted beautiful borders and frames, it would take years to acquire a collection like this. However, with this easy-to-use resource, you'll have them all—right here, right now.

Each image has been reproduced to the highest quality standard for photocopying and scanning; reduce or enlarge them to suit your needs. A CD-Rom containing all of the images in digital form is included, enabling you to use them for any computer project over and again. If you prefer to use them as they're printed, simply cut them out—they're printed on one side only.

Perfect for paper crafting, scrapbooking, and fabric transfers, *Memories of a Lifetime* books will inspire you to explore new avenues of creativity. We've included a sampling of ideas to get you started, but the best part is using your imagination to create your own fabulous projects. Be sure to look for other books in this series as we continue to search the markets for wonderful vintage images.

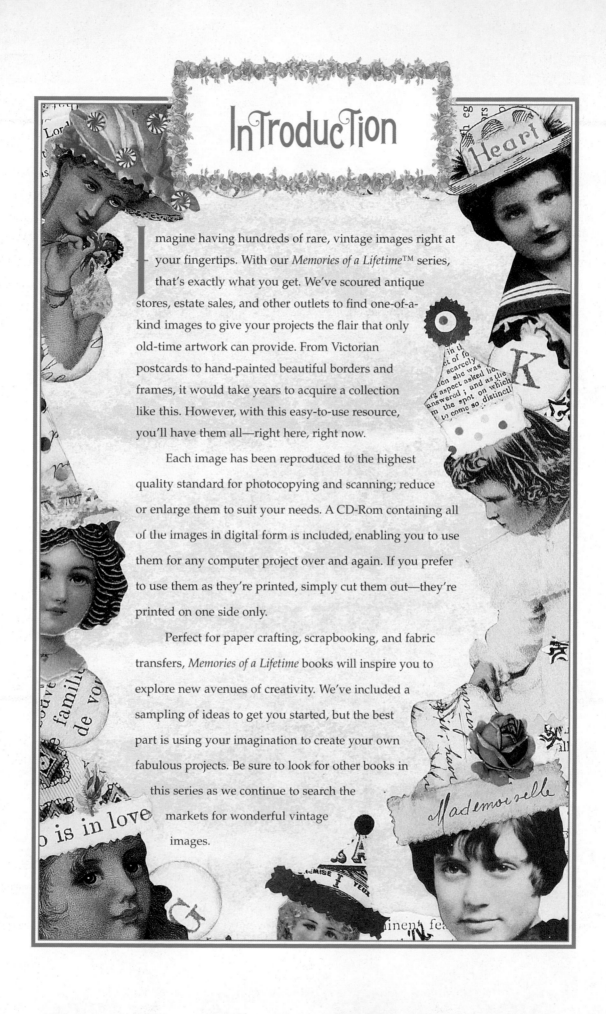

How to
Use This Book

General Instructions:

These images are printed on one side only, making it easy to simply cut out the desired image. However, you'll probably want to use them again, so we have included a CD-Rom which contains all of the images individually as well as in the page layout form. The CDs can be used with both PC and Mac formats. Just pop in the disk. On a PC, the file will immediately open to the Home page, which will walk you through how to view and print the images. For Macintosh® users, you will simply double-click on the icon to open. The images may also be incorporated into your computer projects using simple imaging software that you can purchase specifically for this purpose—a perfect choice for digital scrapbooking.

The reference numbers printed on the back of each image in the book are the same ones used on the CD, which will allow you to easily find the image you are looking for. The numbering consists of the book abbreviation, the page number, the image number, and the file format. The first file number (located next to the page number) is for the entire page. For example, WD01-001.jpg would be the entire image for page 1 of *Weddings*. The second file number is for the top-right image. The numbers continue in a counterclockwise fashion.

Once you have resized your images, added text, created a scrapbook page, etc., you are ready to print them out. Printing on cream or white cardstock, particularly a textured variety, creates a more authentic look. You won't be able to tell that it's a repro-duction! If you don't have access to a computer or printer, that's ok. Most photocopy centers can resize and print your images for a nominal fee, or they have do-it-yourself machines that are easy to use.

Ideas for Using the Images:

Scrapbooking: These images are perfect for both heritage and modern scrapbook pages. Simply use the image as a frame, accent piece, or border. For those of you with limited time, the page layouts in this book have been created so that you can use them as they are. Simply print out or photocopy the desired page, attach a photograph into one of the boxes, and you have a beautiful scrapbook page in minutes. For a little dimension, add a ribbon or charm. Be sure to print your images onto acid-free cardstock so the pages will last a lifetime.

Cards: Some computer programs allow images to be inserted into a card template, simplifying cardmaking. If this is not an option, simply use the images as accent pieces on the front or inside of the card. Use a bone folder to score the card's fold to create a more professional look.

Decoupage/Collage Projects: For decoupage or collage projects, photocopy or print the image onto a thinner paper such as copier paper. Thin paper adheres to projects more effectively. Decoupage medium glues and seals the project, creating a gloss or matte finish when dry, thus protecting the image. Vintage images are beautiful when decoupaged to cigar boxes, glass plates, and even wooden plaques. The possibilities are endless.

Fabric Arts: Vintage images can be used in just about any fabric craft imaginable: wall hangings, quilts, bags, or baby bibs. Either transfer the image onto the fabric by using a special iron-on paper, or by printing the image directly onto the fabric, using a temporary iron-on stabilizer that stabilizes the fabric to feed through a printer. These items are available at most craft and sewing stores. If the item will be washed, it is better to print directly on the fabric. For either method, follow the instructions on the package.

Wood Transfers: It is now possible to "print" images on wood. Use this exciting technique to create vintage plaques, clocks, frames, and more. A simple, inexpensive transfer tool is available at most large craft or home improvement stores, or online from various manufacturers. You simply place the photocopy of the image you want, face down, onto the surface and use the tool to transfer the image onto the wood. This process requires a copy from a laser printer, which means you will probably have to get your copies made at a copy center. Refer to manufacturer's instructions for additional details. There are other transfer products available that can be used with wood. Choose the one that is easiest for you.

Gallery of Ideas

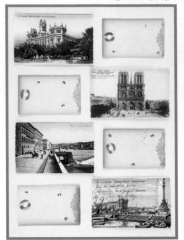

These *Wedding* images can be used in a variety of projects; cards, scrapbook pages, and decoupage projects to name a few. The images can be used as they are shown in the layout, or you can copy and clip out individual images, or even portions or multitudes of images. The following pages contain a collection of ideas to inspire you to use your imagination and create one-of-a-kind treasures.

Honeymoon Scrapbook Page

This page is an example of how you can use a layout straight from the book, and just add your own photography. Use the tags for journaling your trip.

Our view across crystal blue waters—an afternoon walk on Kauna'oa Bay.

Our Honeymoon

The lush and tranquil view from our condo's shaded stoop.

A spectacular sunset in our private Eden.

original page

The artwork in this book can be used to commemorate many events relating to the engagement, wedding, and even honeymoon. A charming vintage label would make a great invitation to a wedding shower, postcard images would make wonderful place cards or tags for thank-you gifts, and the beautiful alphabets can serve as monograms for any of the new couple's correspondence.

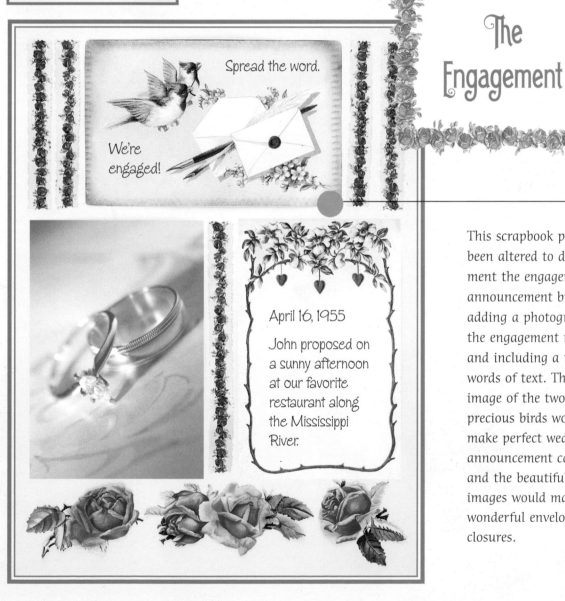

Spread the word.

We're engaged!

April 16, 1955

John proposed on a sunny afternoon at our favorite restaurant along the Mississippi River.

The Engagement

This scrapbook page has been altered to document the engagement announcement by adding a photograph of the engagement ring and including a few words of text. The image of the two precious birds would make perfect wedding announcement cards, and the beautiful rose images would make wonderful envelope closures.

French Floret Tiara

To make this fanciful piece, cut decorative strips of your favorite images from this book. Fold strips in half and glue together to form figure eights. Glue several together to form florets. Add some gathered crepe paper, vintage roses, and a few pearls to the floret centers. Attach to a cardstock band that has been covered front and back with book print. Crepe paper streamers are a wonderful finishing touch.

Vintage Bouquet Holder

This beautiful bouquet holder is made by decoupaging sheet music to a square piece of cardstock and rolling into a cone shape. The edges are glued together and trimmed as necessary.

Various images: roses, scrolls, stamps, etc., can be cut out and glued randomly around the cone. Finish with organza ribbon bows glued to the sides and a bit of antique lace tucked inside.

Wedding Cake Centerpiece

This fabulous centerpiece is made with two different sizes of papier-mâché boxes. The beautiful scrolled alphabets are copied and decoupaged around the boxes. The archway and happy couple are backed with cardstock and glued into place. Doilies, miniature paper fans, and crepe paper balls add the perfect finishing touches.

For this unique piece, create a simple triangular box from cardstock. Decoupage floral print paper onto the box top and sides. Glue desired images to a piece of cardstock and cut out precisely. Decorate the box with the images, using foam dots for dimension.

Keepsake Cake
Wedge Box

Keepsake Place Card Holder

This is a thoughtful way to show relatives where they will be seated at your wedding. If you have a wedding photo of the guests, use that. Otherwise, any photo of them will do. Photocopy the picture in black-and-white to retain the vintage feel.

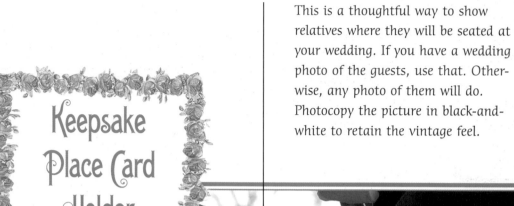

To make this *Keepsake Place Card Holder* glue book print to the inside of a blank card and the script print to front of card. Make a frame using vintage rose images and attach to the front with foam dots. The tiny rolled scroll could be a thank-you note, a copy of the wedding vows, or a favorite quote.

Mother's Gown Scrapbook Page

To make this page, choose your favorite frame image from the book and photocopy it twice. Glue one of the frames to your scrapbook page and use the other to cut out individual images. Attach the images around the frame with foam dots. Embellish with vintage rhinestones, beads, and a ribbon woven through the top edge.

f your being. love is a sacred flame burn- g upon the heart. It is an honor you, young ma and con-

only place is that of the thorn among the roses of life. If one is caught by a pretty face, or an eleg head of hair, or a lovely form, or gay man- of witchery nquired into adaptabil- lock that is . External glitter true and

True love is a sa on the altar of the heart. you, young man, to possess the love ence of an affectionate woman; and to you, young woman, a matter of now that you possess the heart of a tr We can have no patience with the unnatur son, whether male or female trifles w affections of another unpar me to win and finally of ions of wealth or stand pros life. There are clouds eno darken this world. Broken lyres are sc along life's pathway, and it is our duty gathering up only the sunbeams and fr song. While it is true that

Wedding Congratulations

"Into each life some rain must fall, ome days must be dark and d

were only guarded, feelings of oth

he was always ot one of the he always has ne, and when smile and a and she has lay to please eart to speak souls properly ve with each ew beauty to her, and each her. To such rn, garmented fe to the eye, stars." at a married pt to retrieve a single one, ened and re- self-respect all abroad be here is a little

WD01-001

WD02-002

WD02-004   WD02-003

WD02-005   WD02-006

Strolling down a Shady Lane.

While filling up the bag with

WD03-002

WD03-004   WD03-003

WD03-005   WD03-006

3 WD03-001

WD04-001

WD05-002

WD05-003

WD05-004   WD05-010

WD05-005   WD05-007   WD05-009

WD05-006   WD05-008

5 — WD05-001

WD06-002

WD06-004

WD06-003

WD06-005

WD06-006

ended, and in less than two thousand dollars had been

Beaux fiancés que ma tendresse

the fifteenth of October.

Ne m'oubliez pas

N AND ADVANTAGES

spoil the broth." Probably be don'

Jeunes fiancés que vos cœurs

; if the students have fires t is an extra expense, but

The most emin say, "They ar

Amitié

Bonne et Heureuse Année

packages. It is made from selected fruit, a fine quality of sugar, and flavored with pure Vanilla beans. It is a triumph of CHOCOLATE MAKING.

not possible. Its to authors and ar

Si mon bouquet vous fait plaisir,

address for **25 cents**. Liberal terms to agents. | tions, serial sto

WD07-002

WD07-004   WD07-003

WD07-005   WD07-006

7 WD07-001

WD08-002

WD08-003

WD08-004

WD08-008

WD08-005

WD08-006

WD08-007

Ces fleurs sont le meilleur gage de notre amitié

WD09-001

WD10-003

WD10-002

WD10-007

WD10-004

WD10-006

WD10-008

WD10-005

WD10-009

WD10-018

WD10-019

WD10-010

WD10-017

WD10-011

WD10-016

WD10-014

WD10-012

WD10-013

WD10-015

WD10-001 10

Time cannot
change or
alter me,
Whate'er may be
my lot,
My heart will still
be true to thee,—
Then, oh!
Forget-me not

WD11-001

WD12-001

WD13-001

WD14-002

WD14-005　　　　　　WD14-004　　　　　　WD14-003

WD14-008　　　　　　WD14-007　　　　　　WD14-006

WD14-011　　　　　　WD14-010　　　　　　WD14-009

WD14-014　　　　　　WD14-013　　　　　　WD14-012

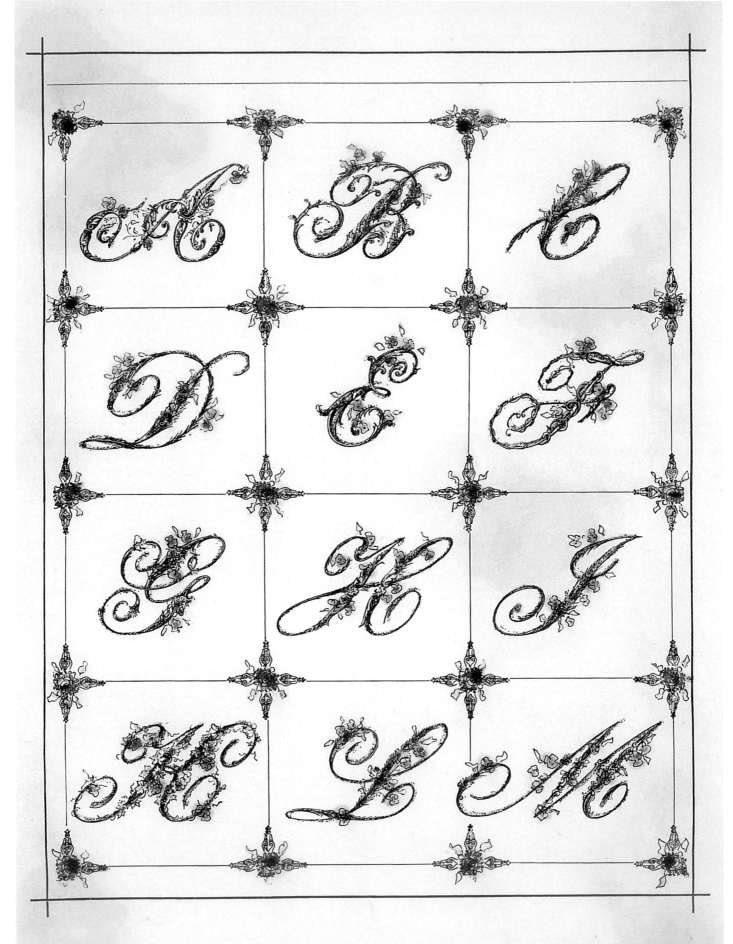

WD15-002

WD15-005   WD15-004   WD15-003

WD15-008   WD15-007   WD15-006

WD15-011   WD15-010   WD15-009

WD15-014   WD15-013   WD15-012

WD16-001

OLD ENGLISH TITLE TEXT.

A B C D E F G H I K L M

N O P Q R S T U V W X Y Z

a b c d e f g h i j k l m n o p q r s t u v w x y z

OLD ENGLISH FANCY TEXT.

A B C D E F G H I J K L M N O P Q

R S V V X Y Z &.

a b c d e f g h i j k l m n o p q r s t u v w x y z.

MEDIEVAL.

A B C D E F G H I J K L M N

O P Q R S T U V W X Y Z &

a b c d e f g h i j k l m n o p q r s t u

v w x y z. 1 2 3 4 5 6 7 8 9 0.

WD17-001

WD18-001

WD19-001

WD20-003

WD20-002

WD20-004

WD20-009

WD20-005

WD20-008

WD20-006

WD20-007

WD21-002

WD21-003

WD21-004

WD21-005

WD22-002

WD22-003

WD22-004   WD22-011

WD22-005   WD22-010

WD22-006   WD22-009

WD22-007   WD22-008

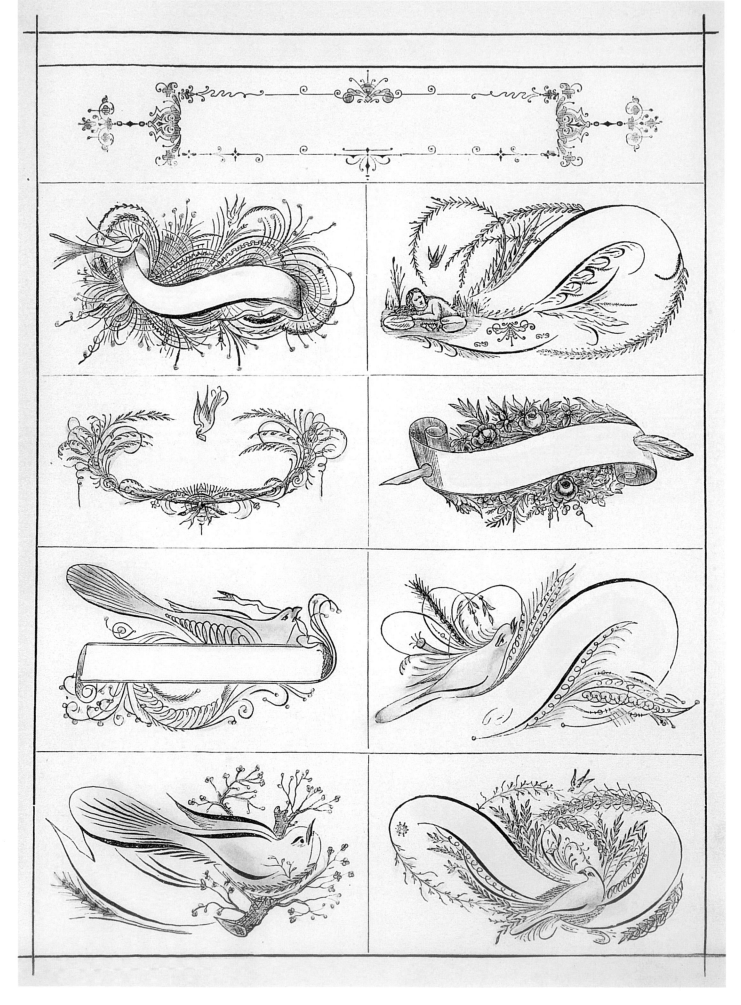

WD23-002

WD23-005   WD23-004   WD23-003

WD23-006   WD23-010

WD23-007

WD23-008   WD23-009

WD24-003

WD24-002

WD24-004

WD24-007

WD24-005

WD24-006

WD25-003   WD25-002

                                                WD25-007

WD25-004

WD25-005   WD25-006

WD26-002

WD26-004   WD26-003

WD26-005   WD26-008

WD26-006   WD26-007

Post Card

CORRESPONDENCE ADD

Carte postale
Brefkort
Karta korespond
universale · Weltp
Cartão postal

Cleopatra—the var
magnificence of its pic
exhibited the characteris

U.S. POSTAGE
ONE CENT

Remember
your
Friend

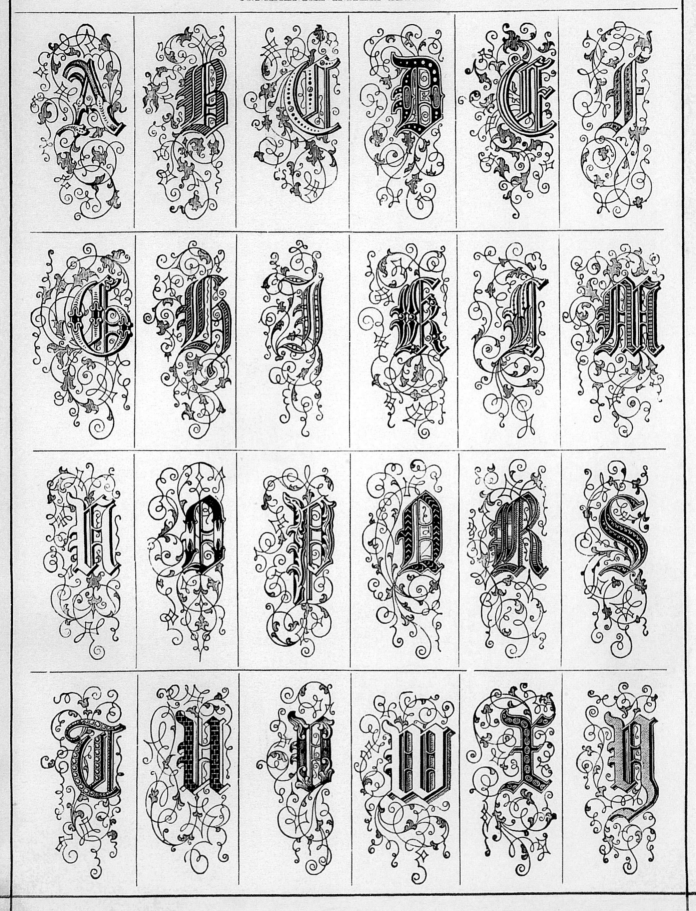

WD27-003

WD27-004

WD27-005

WD27-006

WD27-007

WD27-008

WD27-009

WD27-010

WD27-011

WD27-012

WD27-013

WD27-014

WD27-015

WD27-016

WD27-017

WD27-018

WD27-019

WD27-020

WD27-021

WD27-022

WD27-023

WD27-024

WD27-025

WD27-026

WD28-001

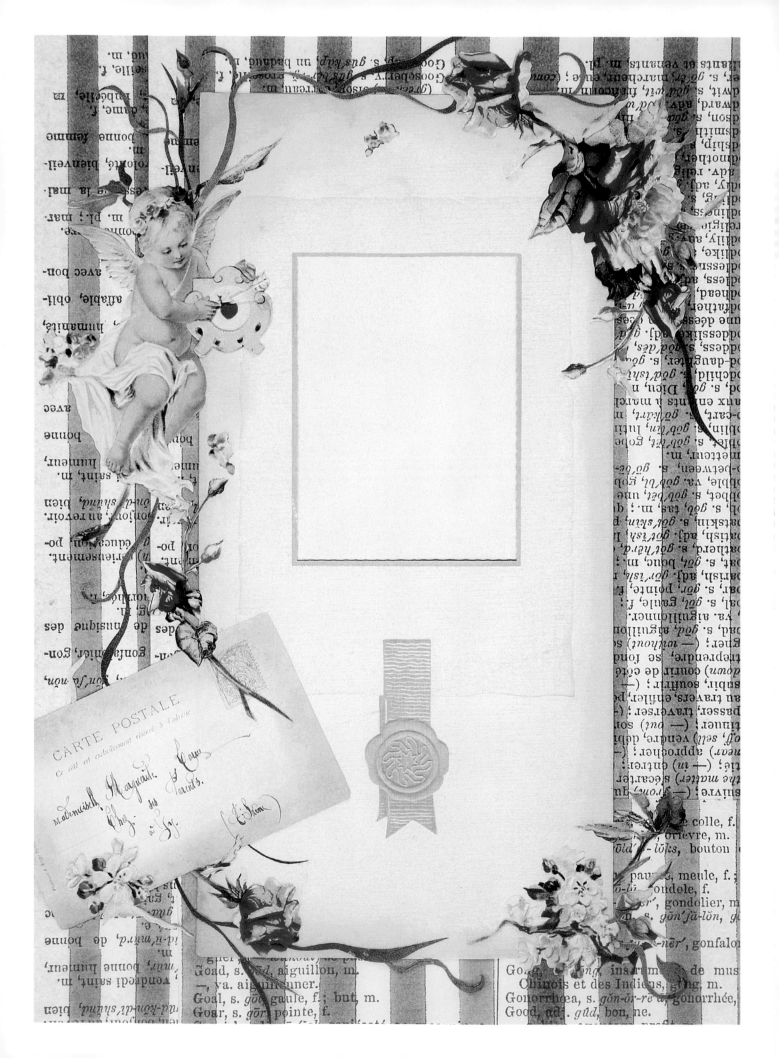

WD29-002

WD29-003

WD29-004

WD30-004

WD30-003

WD30-002

WD30-005

WD30-010

WD30-009

WD30-006

WD30-007

WD30-008

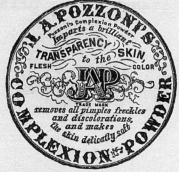

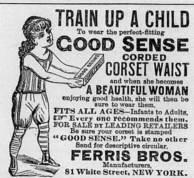
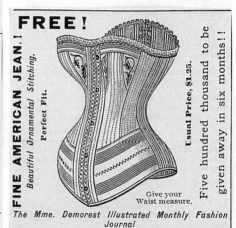

WD31-004   WD31-003   WD31-002

WD31-005   WD31-010   WD31-009

WD31-006   WD31-007   WD31-008

WD31-001

WD32-004   WD32-003   WD32-002

WD32-005   WD32-009   WD32-008

WD32-006   WD32-007

WITH
FONDEST
LOVE.

A Gift
of Love

Truly thine.

Tu m'as donné le grand frisson
Que l'on éprouve sans comprendre,
Tant il est doux, tant il est tendre,
Tant il déroute la raison !

CARTE POSTALE

Ce côté est exclusivement réservé à l'adresse

Merci pour vos souhaits

WD33-003

WD33-002

WD33-004

WD33-007

WD33-005

WD33-006

WD33-001

WD34-006   WD34-005   WD34-004   WD34-003   WD34-002

WD34-009   WD34-008   WD34-007

WD34-013   WD34-012   WD34-011   WD34-010

WD34-018   WD34-017   WD34-016   WD34-015   WD34-014

WD34-021   WD34-020   WD34-019

WD35-001

WD36-002

WD36-004   WD36-003   WD36-010

WD36-009

WD36-005

WD36-006   WD36-008

WD36-007

WD37-001

WD38-001

LE ROI S'AMUSE

4478

TRIBOULET

Ma fille, ô seul bonheur que le ciel m'ait permis,
D'autres ont des parents, des frères, des amis,
Une femme, un mari, des vassaux, un cortège
D'aïeux et d'alliés, plusieurs enfants que sais-je?

4478

TRIBOULET

Scélérats! Assassins! Vous êtes des infâmes
Des voleurs, des bandits, des tourmenteurs de femmes!
Messeigneurs, il me faut ma fille, il me la faut

WD39-002

WD39-004

WD39-003

WD39-005

WD39-006

WD39-001

WD40-004 WD40-003 WD40-002

WD40-005 WD40-011 WD40-010

WD40-006 WD40-009

WD40-007 WD40-008

WD41-002

WD41-003

WD41-004   WD41-008

WD41-005

WD41-006   WD41-007

WD42-001

WD43-003

WD43-005   WD43-004   WD43-002

WD43-006   WD43-010

WD43-007   WD43-009

WD43-008

WD43-001

WD44-005　　　　　　　　　WD44-003　　　　WD44-002

WD44-006　　　　　　　　　　　　WD44-004

WD44-008

WD44-007

CEREMONY

Marriage Notices, etc.

WD45-003   WD45-002

WD45-004

WD45-005

WD45-006   WD45-013

WD45-007

WD45-012

WD45-008   WD45-010   WD45-011

WD45-009

45 — WD45-001

WD46-002

WD46-003   WD46-007   WD46-008

WD46-004   WD46-006

WD46-005

Marriage  License.

—State of—

—County of—

The people of the State of ...., to any person legally authorized to solemnize Marriage, **GREETING:** You are hereby authorized to join in the holy bonds of Matrimony, and to celebrate the rites and ceremonies of Marriage, between Mr. ...., and M ...., according to the usual custom and laws of the State of ...., and you are required to return this license to me within thirty days, from the celebration of such Marriage, with a Certificate of the same, appended thereto, and signed by you, under the penalty of One Hundred Dollars.

Seal.

Witness ...., Clerk of our said Court and the Seal thereof, at his office, in ...., in said County, this day of ...., A.D., ...

.... County Clerk.

State of ...., ... **County.** S.S. I, ... a ...., hereby certify that on the .... day of ...., I joined in Marriage, Mr. ...., and M ...., agreeable to the authority given in the above License, and the customs and laws of this State.

Given under my hand and seal, this .... day of ...., A.D., ...

.... SEAL.

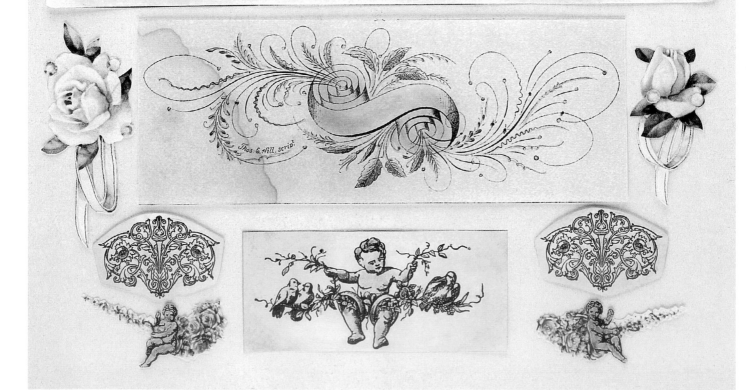

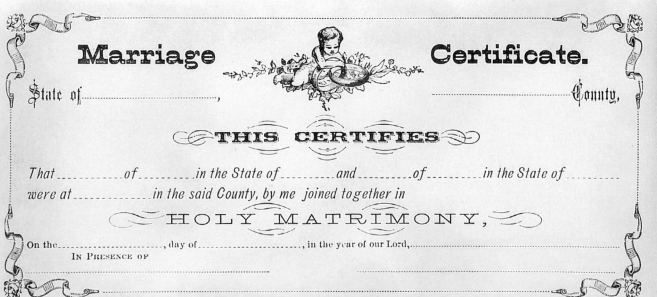

Marriage Certificate.

State of _____, _____ County,

THIS CERTIFIES

That _____ of _____ in the State of _____ and _____ of _____ in the State of _____ were at _____ in the said County, by me joined together in

HOLY MATRIMONY,

On the _____, day of _____, in the year of our Lord, _____

IN PRESENCE OF

_____ _____

_____

WD47-004   WD47-003   WD47-002

WD47-005   WD47-009

WD47-006   WD47-008   WD47-010

WD47-007

WD48-001

WD49-003

WD49-002

WD49-006

WD49-004

WD49-005

WD49-001

WD50-001

The Knightes Tale.   Front.

Best Wishes

The Squieres Tale.   P. 201

WD51-002

WD51-004   WD51-003

WD51-005   WD51-006

WD51-001

WD52-003

WD52-002

WD52-004

WD52-006

WD52-005

WD52-001 — 52

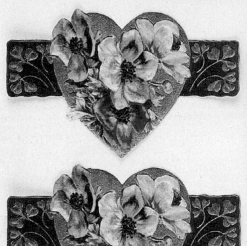

Please...

DO NOT DISTURB

14. MADRID. Salón del Prado y Casa de Correos

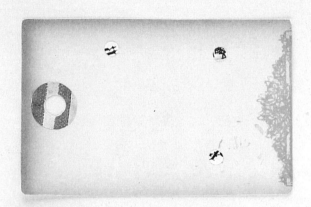

4508 PARIS
Place du Parvis et facade
de Notre-Dame
Style ogival - Construite de 1163 à 1315,
restaurée de 1845 à 1857 par Lassus et
en 1879 par Viollet-le-Duc.

Firenze - Lung' Arno Nuovo

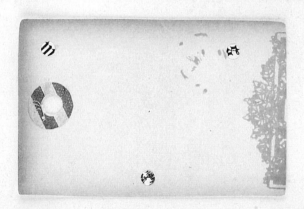

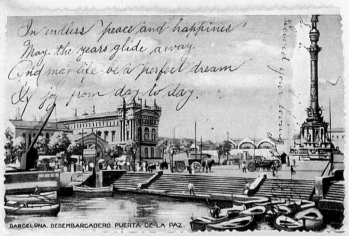

In endless peace and happiness
May the years glide away
And may life be a perfect dream
Of joy from day to day.

BARCELONA. DESEMBARCADERO PUERTA DE LA PAZ.

WD53-003

WD53-002

WD53-004

WD53-009

WD53-005

WD53-008

WD53-006

WD53-007

WD53-001

WD54-001

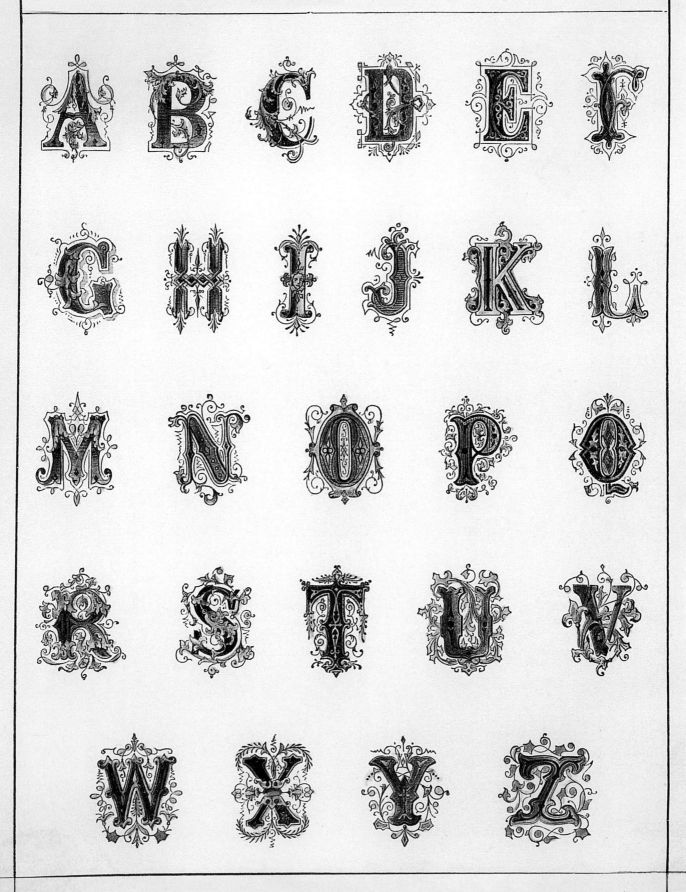

WD55-002

WD55-003

WD55-004

WD55-005

WD55-006

WD55-007

WD55-008

WD55-009

WD55-010

WD55-011

WD55-012

WD55-013

WD55-014

WD55-015

WD55-016

WD55-017

WD55-018

WD55-019

WD55-020

WD55-021

WD55-022

WD55-023

WD55-024

WD55-025

WD55-026

WD55-027

WD55-001

WD56-002

WD56-003

WD56-004

WD56-005

WD56-008

WD56-006

WD56-007

WD56-001 56

Cher Monsieur Vos...

sommes heureux de s...
...us passez votre temps a...
...réablement, profitez en...
...tour vous. nous conter...
...es, sans crainte du scan...
...effraye pas, au cont...
...lles petites poules qui n...
...as être farouches avec...
...s aussi entreprenants...
...Reny, c'est toujours de...
...la pluie que vient...
...nous embêter. Me...
...ous mettre au courant...
...arrose les jardins, je...
...ndis à part les fru...
...a pas grand mal.
...nous aere hier sou...
...s gens que vous reche...
...rce, je pense que cela...
...s rentrer plus tôt; qu...
...ous dire, de vous, Ca...

...fort, aussi Pierre, remet chaque jour a...

WD57-001